LIVING IN GOD'S ECONOMY

McDougal & Associates
Servants of Christ and Stewards of the
Mysteries of God

LIVING IN GOD'S ECONOMY

WHERE IS YOUR MOTIVE, HEART, AND FAITH?

BY

JEREMY F. VOISIN

LIVING IN GOD'S ECONOMY: Where is Your Motive,
Heart, and Faith?
Copyright © 2024—Jeremy F. Voisin
ALL RIGHTS RESERVED

Unless otherwise noted, all Scripture references are from the *Holy Bible, King James Version,* public domain. References marked "NLT" are from the *Holy Bible, New Living Translation,* copyright © 1996, 2004, 2007 by Tyndale House Foundation. Used by permission of Tyndale House Publishers, Inc., Carol Stream, Illinois. References marked "NKJV" are from *The Holy Bible, New King James Version*, copyright © 1979, 1980, 1982, 1990 by Thomas Nelson, Inc., Nashville, Tennessee. References marked "NIV" are from *The Holy Bible, New International Version*, copyright © 1973, 1978, 1984, 2011 by Biblica, Colorado Springs, Colorado. References marked "TLB" are from *The Living Bible* paraphrased by Kenneth Taylor, copyright © 1971 by Tyndale House Publishers, Inc., Wheaton, Illinois. Used by permission. All rights reserved.

Cover photo by the author.

Published by:

McDougal & Associates
www.ThePublishedWord.com

McDougal & Associates is an organization dedicated to spreading the Gospel of the Lord Jesus Christ to as many people as possible in the shortest time possible.

ISBN: 978-1-950398-82-9

Printed on demand in the U.S., the UK, and Australia
For Worldwide Distribution

Acknowledgments

I would like to thank:

Kim and Vanessa Voisin, my parents, for their continued support and leadership. You have never given up on me and continue to encourage me to be successful.

Crystal Callais and her husband, Rusty, for their hard work in helping me get this book onto paper. I would recommend checking out Crystal's books on Amazon. She has a journal, a devotional, and several teaching books.

My faithful wife, Autumn Voisin, for her continued support. You have been with me through the toughest battles.

Contents

Introduction 9

1. Is the Prosperity Gospel Legitimate? 15
2. What Is My Motive? 27
3. Where Is My Heart? 37
4. Hundredfold Faith 47
5. The Activators 59
6. Conclusion 129
   About the Author 133
   Author Contact Page 135

But seek ye first the kingdom of God, and his righteousness; and all these things shall be added unto you.
— Matthew 6:33

INTRODUCTION

One day my pastor approached me about giving a three-to five-minute message on tithes while the offering was being received on Sunday mornings. Following that short message, I would then pray over the congregation the Word I had received from the Lord. That sounds pretty simple. But I remember having an unsettling feeling within and just wanting to say no, not me. Tithing was not my subject, nor did I want to sound like some salesperson asking the congregation to give.

It was not that I didn't believe in giving tithes. I just didn't want to be the one telling other people they should be giving. Besides, there didn't seem to be a lot I could say on the subject, or so I thought at the time. I had very little understanding of the subject of tithing at this point in my life. Yes, I was being personally obedient in that regard, but I was only doing it out of a traditional and religious sense. But I *had* made a commitment to God to say yes to whatever door He opened for me, so, with a grinchy smile, I answered, "Sure, Pastor. I'll be glad to."

At that moment, I embarked on a journey that was to shape, not only my faith in tithing, but in the understanding that our God is a rewarder. Hebrews 11, also known as the faith chapter, says that without faith it is impossible to please God. Anyone who wants to come to Him must believe that He exists and that He rewards those who sincerely seek Him (see Hebrews 11:6).

Early on, the Bible tells the story of two brothers—Cain and Abel. Both of these brothers brought their offering to God, but only one of them pleased Him and found favor with Him. That story had always interested me because they were both following the same religious tradition, but only one of them was accepted by God. Verse 4 of Hebrews 11 clarifies this story by saying:

> *It was by faith that Abel brought a more acceptable offering to God than Cain did.* (NLT)

INTRODUCTION

Our faith, expressed in our actions, is what pleases God. Our obedience cannot be simply from a traditional or religious sense. If we give for that reason, we are being obedient to tradition or religion, and not to God Himself.

In Hosea 6:6, God said:

> *For I desired mercy, and not sacrifice; and the knowledge of God more than burnt offerings.*

This is where I was. Even though I was being obedient to what was physically asked of me, I lacked faith in what I was doing. I didn't have a solid foundation rooted in the Scriptures when it came to the subject of tithing. But, as Romans 10:17 shows, *"Faith comes by hearing and hearing by the word of God"* (NKJV). As I began to study the Scriptures to know which ones to teach on and to confess over my own tithes and those of the rest of the congregation, I began to see a dramatic change, not only in my finances, but also in my trust in God to be my personal Provider.

Before I began this journey, I had been living paycheck to paycheck, seemingly spinning my wheels. I'm not saying that I wasn't blessed; I was just working very hard and feeling as though I couldn't get anywhere financially. Like so many others, I was in debt. I had projected that it would take me the next twenty years to pay off our house, I was able to keep only a few thousand dollars in my checking account at any one time, and I was driving an old beat-up truck so that I could afford more for our growing family.

My beautiful wife and I have five children, and they needed clothing, food, and many other things. How would I ever get ahead? My problem was not a lack of effort; it was a lack of faith. Once I began to learn and then confess God's Word over myself, prosperity began to overflow my life seemingly overnight.

Five years have passed since I began this journey. I can now say that I am debt free. Our house is paid off, and we have been able to purchase two other houses as rental properties. We now have enough money in savings that if I lost my job, I could wait an entire year before I needed to return to work. Please believe me when I say I am not boasting. I'm giving you a testimony of how great our God is and how much He wants to reward us.

INTRODUCTION

Granted, our financial success did not come without hard work, but when I began to confess God's words over my labor, everything I put my hand to prospered.

Hebrews 1:1 declares:

> *Faith is the substance of things hoped for, the evidence of things not seen. For by it the elders obtained a good report.* Hebrews 11:1-2

When we put our faith in God, we are looking toward what His Word says about us. Even when that evidence is not yet seen, we place our faith in His Word, we confess His Word over our situation, and that hope activates God's authority in our lives. It is then that we obtain *"a good report."*

My heart for this book is to aid in building your faith in tithing and for you to become a resource to teach others. We all want to have a good understanding of God's Word so that our seed does not fall by the wayside. When that happens, as Jesus stated in Matthew 13:19, *"The wicked one"* comes and snatches the seed away before it can bear fruit. Why does this happen?

Because we have not had an understanding of God's promises.

Do you have a solid understanding of what the Scriptures say about tithing and giving and God's promise to you in that regard? I invite you to join me on this journey to discover the power of *Living in God's Economy.*

Jeremy Voisin
Montegut, Louisiana

Chapter 1

IS THE PROSPERITY GOSPEL LEGITIMATE?

I want to begin by answering the question: Is the modern prosperity gospel a false doctrine? However, before I get into this subject, I would like you to understand the reasons I feel qualified to speak on this matter.

First, I have never received payment from the offering bucket for preaching or participating in any church service. On one occasion, payment was offered to me for preaching a sermon during a Sunday service, and I did receive the check, but afterward, I decided to sow it into the church building fund. I'm not saying that we should not pay our ministers. As Paul said, in 1 Timothy 5:18, *"The laborer is worthy of his wages"* (NKJV).

LIVING IN GOD'S ECONOMY

The second reason I feel qualified to write and speak on this subject is my personal testimony. Before I discovered these principles, I was in financial debt, and now I'm not. We all have times in our life when money is tight. If that's where you find yourself, don't condemn yourself. Allow the Holy Spirit to open your eyes to the concepts in this book. I truly believe that if you apply the Word of God to your situation, that situation will change.

God's Word is powerful when we believe it and apply it through a generous heart and a right spirit. We overcome *"by the word of [our] testimony"* (Revelation 12:11). What are you speaking over your finances? These truths have become real to me through experience:

> *Then he [Jesus] told them a story: "A rich man had a fertile farm that produced fine crops. He said to himself, 'What should I do? I don't have room for all my crops.' Then he said, 'I know! I'll tear down my barns and build bigger ones. Then I'll have room enough to store all my wheat and other goods. And I'll sit back and say to myself, "My friend, you have enough stored away for*

Is the Prosperity Gospel Legitimate?

years to come. Now take it easy! Eat, drink, and be merry!"'

"But God said to him, 'You fool! You will die this very night. Then who will get everything you worked for?'

"Yes, a person is a fool to store up earthly wealth but not have a rich relationship with God."

Luke 12:16-21, NLT

Prosperity should never be our focus; our focus should be on Kingdom building and our relationship with our heavenly Father. This is fundamental to not letting the cares of this world, the deceitfulness of riches, and the lust of other things enter in, choking the Word and making it unfruitful (see Matthew 13:22).

There is what I call a "far right" and a "far left" teaching on this subject of prosperity through tithes and offerings. In the far-right teaching, preachers use the Gospel as a means to gain wealth. Those who do this have tarnished the Gospel and have given the world a reason to mock the Church.

At my place of work, the TV was kept on an outdoors hunting and fishing channel. Every morning a certain TV evangelist would come on and teach on giving to his ministry. He would say, "If you give today, God has a special blessing for you." Hearing this, the people in the room would mock him. "Here we go again," they would say, and I couldn't blame them. This man was like a salesman or a con artist, trying to deceive people to get their money. When I heard it, anger would rise in me toward him. If I could, I would have climbed through the TV and punched him in the face.

People like that are on the far right of the prosperity gospel, and I question their relationship with the Father. They are using the biblical truths of the Gospel as a sales pitch to get people to give. Jesus taught in the Sermon on the Mount:

> *Lay not up for yourselves treasures upon earth, where moth and rust doth corrupt, and where thieves break through and steal: but lay up for yourselves treasures in heaven, where neither moth nor rust doth corrupt, and where thieves do not break through nor steal: for where your treasure is, there will your heart be also.* Matthew 6:19-21

Our focus must be on Kingdom building. I would remind preachers like these that Jesus

Is the Prosperity Gospel Legitimate?

overturned the tables in the Temple and cast out the merchants. Repent now before you, too, are cast out.

Then there are those who are on the far left of the issue. They claim that prosperity preaching is a false doctrine, that it is a misinterpretation of the Scriptures. I appreciate these guys for their desire for the authenticity of scripture. I personally would rather be in this camp than on the side of the TV salesmen. But these lefties are so far left on the issue that they believe the Old Testament was only written for the children of Israel and has no application today. Sure, it was for that time. I agree. But it is also valid for us today as well.

Those generations had only the Old Testament. We have both the Old Testament and the New Testament and can see that Jesus fulfilled the righteous requirements of the Old. For example, we no longer sacrifice animals for the forgiveness of sins, but the promises of God found throughout the Old Testament remain. God did not change His mind about how He behaves toward His children. Why would God want to bless those who loved Him and kept His commandments in the Old

Testament and not bless those who love Him and keep His commandments today?

3 John 1:2 states His attitude:

Beloved, I wish above all things that thou mayest prosper and be in health, even as thy soul prospereth.

The patriarchs of the Old Testament were sometimes wealthy and sometimes not, but they were never forsaken. We serve a loving Father who wants to bless His children. But like any good father, He will not give you something that might hurt or destroy you. If prosperity would consume you, then why would our heavenly Father give you wealth?

If you hold this leftist position against prosperity preaching, you must hold the same view on those who preach healing. That makes God a Father who doesn't care about the needs of His children, and that clearly is not true.

Jesus teaches us in Matthew 6 that the heavenly Father knows our needs. If He cares for the lilies in the field, Jesus said, and the birds of the air, how much more important are we to Him? Therefore,

> GOD DID NOT CHANGE HIS MIND ABOUT HOW HE BEHAVES TOWARD HIS CHILDREN!

He concluded, we must seek first the Kingdom of Heaven and His righteousness, and His promise is that *"all these things* [that we need] *shall be added unto you"* (Matthew 6:33).

Godly prosperity is not measured by the quantity of things we own but rather by our having a sound mind, peace in our homes, our physical and spiritual needs met, and the ability to leave an inheritance for our children.

Enjoying godly prosperity does not mean that I will no longer go through trials. I may go through the valley, but I won't stay there. Jesus said that in this life we will face persecution. *"But,"* He said, *"be of good cheer; I have overcome the world"* (John 16:33).

We may face hard times, but we will do so with encouragement. We most certainly will go through some storms, but as we do, we are being refined and prepared for eternity with God.

We are all learning to trust in Him, whether we are believing for the ability to pay a bill, for the healing of a disease, or for some other need. Our faith is growing through every trial we walk in and through.

I am convinced that David's experience of God delivering him from the lion and the bear grew his

Is the Prosperity Gospel Legitimate?

faith to the place where he could defeat the giant he next faced in life. This is the same growing experience we must all go through. Those who allow their faith to grow are the ones who will defeat the giants they face.

Prosperity is a little thing to God. It's a means to teach us how to trust in Him and to believe for the greater works He has promised. But in order to get godly prosperity activated in your life, you must speak God's Word over your situation. By doing this, you experience the authority of God in that situation, and that experience builds your faith.

If God healed you from a fatal disease that had no known cure, that experience would be unforgettable. That would impact you so dramatically that your faith in God as Healer would come easily. And so it is with finances. We grow from faith to faith through every trial and test.

I know what might be going through your mind as you read these words: "But what about the believer who had faith in a situation but never received what he or she was believing for?" We may not know the whole story, and we cannot often see from God's full perspective. Our flesh cannot comprehend God's ways because they are so much higher than our ways (see Isaiah 55: 8-9). Let God be true and every man a liar. If He said it, let's dare to believe it.

The enemy wants you to believe that God doesn't want to heal you or to prosper you, thus causing your faith not to grow. But when we start believing God for the little things, it starts activating His Word, resulting in our faith building in the area we are believing for.

As you will see, my position on tithes is centered on having the right motive,[1] having a heart for the Kingdom, and learning to trust God fully.

There are many benefits besides prosperity that come from being a tither, and there is no downside. What I am presenting to you are the reasons and blessings that come from being a tither.

Take a moment with the Holy Spirit and ask Him to reveal to you your motive, your heart posture, and where your faith lies in regard to this subject of tithing and giving. How well do you walk in the favor and authority of God? You may evaluate yourself and feel you are already on this journey. That's great! But if you evaluated yourself and you feel this is an area of weakness, say a

---

1. Motive: Your reason for doing something. Vocabulary.com

Is the Prosperity Gospel Legitimate?

prayer, asking the Holy Spirit to open the eyes and ears of your heart in a way that you can see and understand the principles of the tithe.

Then ask the Holy Spirit for ways to help you activate and start applying that which He shows you, as you spend some quiet time in His presence. Let's move ahead now as we discover the power of *Living in God's Economy.*

Chapter 2

WHAT IS MY MOTIVE?

Have you ever asked yourself, "What is my motive for giving tithes and offerings?" It's a healthy question to ask. Then, when you have asked, be willing to hear what the Holy Spirit answers. If your actions are to be pleasing to God and you desire to find favor in His sight, then you simply must search your heart and find your true intent.

Genesis 4 records that classic example:

> *Now Adam knew Eve his wife, and she conceived and bore Cain, and said, "I have acquired a man from the LORD." Then she bore again, this time his brother Abel. Now Abel was a keeper of sheep, but Cain was a tiller of the ground. And in the process of time, it came to pass that Cain brought an offering of the fruit of the*

> *ground to the LORD. Abel also brought of the firstborn of his flock and of their fat. And the LORD respected Abel and his offering, but He did not respect Cain and his offering. And Cain was very angry, and his countenance fell.*
>
> *So, the LORD said to Cain, "Why are you angry? And why has your countenance fallen? If you do well, will you not be accepted? And if you do not do well, sin lies at the door. And its desire is for you, but you should rule over it."*
>
> Genesis 4:1-6, NKJV

The interesting thing about this story is that only one of the offerings given to God pleased Him. What was it that Abel did that was different from Cain? It's an important question because it caused Abel to obtain God's favor. I believe the big difference lay in the motive of each of them for offering to God.

Abel gave of *"the firstborn of his flock and of their fat."* This shows that he gave of the very best he had to offer. That sounds like he wanted to impress God. Giving his best meant that he believed what he was doing to be important. He placed value in his offering by giving the very best.

What is My Motive?

Being a South Louisiana man, my Cajun wife loves to eat blue pinch crabs. So, I will go occasionally to my secret spots and catch her some. To impress my beautiful wife, I also must feed our five children. After catching enough blue pinch crabs to feed my entire family, I then cook up a traditional Cajun meal. Bon appetite!

But, before serving the rest of the family, I pick out two or three of the biggest and fattest crabs and take these hand-selected ones, the best out of the entire catch, and place them on my wife's plate. What better way to score points with a Cajun woman!

My wife always gives me a big smile and blows me a kiss of approval, showing that my offering has been accepted. Why did I pick out the very best crabs for her? Because I had faith that this would impress her and show her just how valuable she is to me. It shows her that I am putting her first and that I want her to have my best.

Hebrews 11:4 (NLT) says, *"It was by faith that Abel brought to God a more acceptable offering than Cain did."* Abel's giving of his firstborn and of their fat showed his faith in what he was doing. It shows that he wanted to prove to God that He was first in his life and that he wanted to give Him the very best.

Genesis 4 says, *"Cain brought of the fruit of the ground an offering unto the L*ORD*."* To my way of thinking, there is an emphasis on the words *"an offering."* I personally feel that it could have been a very different story if it were said of Cain that he brought the first and best of his fruits and the ripest of his harvests. But, no. He brought only *an offering.* That leads me to believe that he was doing this out of obligation and simply as a religious act. There was nothing about his sacrifice that demonstrated significance. It was just *an offering.*

King David needed a piece of land to build an altar and present his offering to God. When Araunah, the Jebusite, was trying to give King David everything he needed to make the offering to the Lord, David replied, *""No, I insist on buying it, for I will not present burnt offerings to the Lord my God that have cost me nothing"* (2 Samuel 24:24, NLT). It seems that King David understood that giving an offering to God was not to be taken lightly or nonchalantly. If it did not cost him anything, then what value was he offering? David put respect and importance

What is My Motive?

on his action because he put a price on his offering.

I also think of the widow who gave two mites, as referenced in Luke 21. Jesus recognized her giving and said that she had given *"more than anyone else."* Wow! What a statement! This widow had given from what she needed, not out of her excess. These funds would have made a noticeable difference in her day-to-day living. You don't give what you need unless that which you are giving toward is more important than your own need.

For this widow to give her two mites meant that she would have to put her trust in God to meet her needs. Even though she didn't have much, she was willing to show God her love and obedience. Those two mites may have been insignificant in earthly value, but they most definitely were significant in heavenly value. The fact that her offering caught Jesus' attention attests to this fact.

In Luke 7 is another great example of motive. A Pharisee asked Jesus to dine with him in his home. Jesus, accepting this invitation, went to his home and sat down to eat:

LIVING IN GOD'S ECONOMY

When a certain immoral woman from that city heard he was eating there, she brought a beautiful alabaster jar filled with expensive perfume [worth a year's wages in that time]. *Then she knelt behind him at his feet, weeping. Her tears fell on his feet, and she wiped them off with her hair. Then she kept kissing his feet and putting perfume on them.*

When the Pharisee who had invited him saw this, he said to himself, "If this man were a prophet, he would know what kind of woman is touching him. She is a sinner!"

Then Jesus answered his thoughts. "Simon," he said to the Pharisee, "I have something to say to you."

"Go ahead, Teacher," Simon replied.

Luke 7:37-40, NLT

Then Jesus told Simon this story:

"A man loaned money to two people—500 pieces of silver to one and 50 pieces to the other. But neither of them could repay him, so he kindly forgave them both, canceling their debts. Who do you suppose loved him more after that?"

What is My Motive?

Simon answered, "I suppose the one for whom he canceled the larger debt."

"That's right," Jesus said. Then he turned to the woman and said to Simon, "Look at this woman kneeling here. When I entered your home, you did not offer me water to wash the dust from my feet, but she has washed them with her tears and wiped them with her hair. You did not greet me with a kiss, but from the time I first came in, she has not stopped kissing my feet. You neglected the courtesy of olive oil to anoint my head, but she has anointed my feet with rare perfume.

"I tell you, her sins—and they are many—have been forgiven, so she has shown me much love. But a person who is forgiven little shows only little love."

Then Jesus said to the woman, "Your sins are forgiven." Luke 7:412-47, NLT

I can only imagine how Simon must have felt at this point—horrible. Even though he had invited Jesus into his home for dinner, his inward motives were exposed by his actions. That alabaster jar symbolized giving God our best and our all. This was Mary's way of bringing her best. She didn't bring the least of what she had or what she figured she could live without; she brought her absolute best, and her offering was purely out of love.

These stories reveal the motives of various people and how they responded to an offering. Their actions exposed the motive of their heart. Like Abel, giving God the first of his increase, or like David, wanting his offering to cost him something, and like the widow who was willing to trust God in her poverty. It was not the amount given that was important; the importance lay in the heart motive.

So how does this relate to us today? It's not as if we can physically wash Jesus's feet or perform a burnt offering as of old. We demonstrate our love for God through our prayer life, through our devotion to His Word, through being a servant in His Kingdom, through living a holy life, and through our tithes and offerings to the church.

Our motive in giving the tithe, ten percent of our increase, should be out of love for God and seeing His Kingdom advance. When this is true, when our heart is in the right place, our gift becomes more than just *an offering*.

IT WAS NOT THE AMOUNT GIVEN THAT WAS IMPORTANT; THE IMPORTANCE LAY IN THE HEART MOTIVE!

You might ask, "How is paying tithes to the church demonstrating my love for God?" Before we dive further into this topic in the following chapter, I want to leave you with this thought. Jesus said, *"Where your treasure is, there your heart will be also"* (Matthew 6:21 and Luke 12:34). What is it that you treasure most?

Let us take a moment and ask the Holy Spirit to reveal the intent or motive of our heart. Ask yourself: Is my motive in giving the tithe to get more riches? Am I looking for recognition among men? Do I feel or act out of obligation by religious tradition? Do I treat God like a waitress offering Him a tip?

The definition for *motive,* again, is "a reason for doing something, causing movement or action."[1] We often hear of motive in the context of a crime. A suspect's fingerprints may be on the murder weapon, but you cannot really understand the crime until you understand the motive behind it. What made the killer act?

Your fingerprints are all over your tithes, but what is the thing that moves you to sow into the offering basket? Now we are going deeper to discover the power of *Living in God's Economy.*

---

1   Vocabulary.com

Chapter 3

WHERE IS MY HEART
(Is God's Kingdom My Treasure?)

I would like to tell my own parable from a Cajun perspective. The Kingdom of Heaven is like a good old Cajun fisherman named Boudreaux. Old Boudreaux went out fishing one day, and he became lost. While trying to find his way home, he discovered a bayou that he had never seen before. Out of curiosity, Boudreaux cast his fishing line in to see if there were any fish. As soon as his line touched the water, he caught a beautiful redfish. He tried again, and with every cast he would bring in another beautiful redfish.

After catching his limit of redfish, old Boudreaux decided to go throw his cast net, to see if there were any shrimp. Sure enough, in his first cast, he brought into the boat a net full of shrimp. This had him very excited.

Next old Boudreaux decided to try to catch some crabs. He set out one crab trap, and to his surprise caught more crabs than his trap could hold. At this point, he rushed home to show his wife what he had discovered.

Boudreaux and his wife became so excited that they sold everything they owned and bought that fishing spot. There, right in the spot where Boudreaux had experienced that great catch, they built themselves a lovely little home.

When we get a revelation of the Kingdom of Heaven, all earthly possessions pale in comparison. In that moment, the only thing that really matters is possessing the Kingdom.

Just take a moment to reflect on the magnitude of Heaven and its glory. How can you compare eternity to this mortal life? It is like comparing a job that pays $1.00 an hour to another job that pays $1,000,000 an hour. It's so foolish for anyone to think that this mortal life is more valuable than eternity. I would rather store up my treasures in Heaven for eternity than to hold on to treasures in this mortal life that is so quickly passing away.

I WOULD RATHER STORE UP MY TREASURES IN HEAVEN FOR ETERNITY THAN TO HOLD ON TO TREASURES IN THIS MORTAL LIFE THAT IS SO QUICKLY PASSING AWAY!

Holding on to the treasures of this world is like a man who is buying into the stock market for his retirement. Let's say he has been investing and buying shares of a company that is going bankrupt. When it comes time for his retirement, he then discovers that all his investments are of no value. How sad would that day be for him?

What if that was you? What if you thought you were setting yourself and your family up for retirement, only to later discover that you had no retirement savings at all?

Jesus is preparing a place for us that is so glorious we cannot even fathom what it will truly be like. Nothing this world can offer will compare. It's like Paul said in Romans 8:18:

> *Yet what we suffer now is nothing compared to the glory he will reveal to us later.* (NLT)

Having this type of attitude is what we refer to as being "Kingdom minded." The Kingdom of Heaven is the greatest treasure one could ever hope to obtain. It is worth everything, and nothing—absolutely nothing—can compare to its value. When we give our tithes, we are sowing into this heavenly Kingdom. Our giving is an outward sign of an inward commitment.

Your tithes place value on your heart's desire for the Kingdom. Again, as Jesus said in (Matthew 6:21):

> *Where your treasure is there your heart will be also.*

Let me be very honest with you. My flesh does not ever want to give money away. My flesh loves the things of this world, and money is the means of satisfying those desires. The practice of giving my tithe to the Kingdom crucifies my flesh, bringing it into submission to my heart's desire. This is what Jesus meant when He said, *"Seek ye first the kingdom of God and His righteousness"* (Matthew 6:33, NKJV).

There are many reasons I could give you for investing our tithes in God's Kingdom, but my best reason is LOVE. I am in love with God and in love with His Kingdom. Being reminded of the Parable of the Hidden Treasure (see Matthew 13:44), I found my treasure, and I am willing to

WHEN WE GIVE OUR TITHES, WE ARE SOWING INTO THIS HEAVENLY KINGDOM. OUR GIVING IS AN OUTWARD SIGN OF AN INWARD COMMITMENT!

WHERE IS MY HEART

sell everything I have to possess it. When I tithe, I see God taking my finite[1] resources and using them to expand His Kingdom. In this way, I become a partner with Him in His work. It is like Jesus taking the five loaves and two fish offered by a little boy and feeding five thousand. God can take my finite resource and multiply it five thousand times.

I can imagine that boy walking around so proud of himself for having been part of feeding that multitude. When we partner with God, we find ourselves in the same position as that boy. God is taking our five loaves and two fish that are finite and feeding the multitude. I don't know about you, but that sounds like a good deal to me.

Paul said in Galatians 6:8:

For he that soweth to his flesh shall reap corruption; but he that soweth to the Spirit shall of the Spirit reap life everlasting.

Jesus said in Luke 16:9:

And I say unto you, Make to yourselves friends of the mammon of unrighteousness; that, when

---
1. Finite: Having a limited nature or existence. Miriam Webster Dictionary

ye fail, they may receive you into everlasting habitations.

Through our tithes, we are partnering with Kingdom work.

In writing to the Philippian believers, Paul described our giving as *"an odour of a sweet smell, a sacrifice acceptable, wellpleasing to God"* (Philippians 4:18).

Philippians 4 reveals that the Philippian church was sending financial support to Paul. He said that because of their giving, they had *"communicated"* with his *"necessity"* (verses 14 and 15). In other words, they became partakers together of Paul's labor. In verse 17 of that chapter, he revealed that the actions of the Philippians were increasing their heavenly account. Think about it. Even though you might not be a pastor or a missionary, you can partner with them in their labors by your financial support. Their accomplishments are then added to your eternal rewards.

In Malachi 3:10, God said:

> *Bring ye all the tithes into the storehouse, that there may be meat in mine house.*

WHERE IS MY HEART

The word *meat* here is referring to food and originates from a word meaning "to provide food." Your tithe is providing the needs of the church.

Always remember: it is God that gives you the power to get wealth, that He may establish His covenant (see Deuteronomy 8:18). For me, this is reason enough to be a tither, simply because it is pleasing to my King. My giving is a sweet smell to my Father. Nothing is more gratifying than to know that I am partnering with Kingdom work with my finite resources, that my giving is facilitating the Gospel being preached, and those who receive the Good News become my friends and will receive me into everlasting habitation.

Are you putting your eyes on eternity and not in this present mortal world? It gets even better. Let's continue to go deeper to discover the power of *Living in God's Economy*.

NOTHING IS MORE GRATIFYING THAN TO KNOW THAT I AM PARTNERING WITH KINGDOM WORK WITH MY FINITE RESOURCES, THAT MY GIVING IS FACILITATING THE GOSPEL BEING PREACHED!

Chapter 4

FAITH FOR THE HUNDREDFOLD RETURN

Before I began teaching on the tithe, my faith on this subject was quite small. I was basing my faith and understanding on just a few scriptures. Since it was not a subject I taught on regularly, I had never really meditated on God's Word on this matter. I was just being obedient to the pastor I was under, and my faith at the time was limited to Malachi 3.

Knowing that God said to bring the tithe into the storehouse and that, in return, He would bless my finances if I did, I had been content with that basic understanding. And that's not really a bad place to be. I was being obedient, and I had faith that God was blessing my obedience. I believe my heart was in the right place, and I was giving because I wanted to see the Kingdom of God advance.

God was blessing me, and Malachi 3 was operating in my life, but when I had to begin teaching on tithes and had to search out more Bible truths on the subject, something changed in my faith. I watched as God began to move in greater ways than ever before in my finances.

Jesus said:

> *But these are the ones sown on good ground, those who hear the word, accept it, and bear fruit: some thirtyfold, some sixty, and some a hundred.*
> Mark 4:20, NKJV

According to this scripture, when you sow, you can reap thirty, sixty, or a hundredfold. There are distinct levels of return. Just because you are accepting the Word of God and exercising your faith does not mean that you will automatically get a hundredfold return of the fruit which it can produce. But this is what I began to experience as I stepped out in obedience, stretching my faith and beginning to teach on the subject of tithes.

WHEN I HAD TO BEGIN TEACHING ON TITHES AND HAD TO SEARCH OUT MORE BIBLE TRUTHS ON THE SUBJECT, SOMETHING CHANGED IN MY FAITH!

The more I taught on what God has said on the matter, the more it began to take root deeper in me than ever before. I began to confess God's Word over my life, and the result was that I started to recognize God's blessing over my life. His Word was building up my faith. As my faith grew, I started going from a thirtyfold increase, to sixtyfold, and now I find myself at the hundredfold return level.

Please realize that I am not making this statement out of pride, and I certainly am not boasting of my ability. I am boasting on God and His principles. His Word was renewing my mind every time I opened it to read, bringing me into a higher relationship and authority with and through Him. I believe with everything that is within me that when you start activating God's Word in any area, you will become more victorious than you previously were.

Hebrews 11:6 tells us:

> *But without faith it is impossible to please Him, for he who comes to God must believe that He is, and that He is a rewarder of those who diligently seek Him.* (NKJV)

As my faith grew, I started going from a thirtyfold increase, to sixtyfold, and now I find myself at the hundredfold return level!

I BELIEVE WITH EVERYTHING THAT IS WITHIN ME THAT WHEN YOU START ACTIVATING GOD'S WORD IN ANY AREA, YOU WILL BECOME MORE VICTORIOUS THAN YOU PREVIOUSLY WERE!

Faith for the Hundredfold Return

In this current season of my life, I am learning to see God as a rewarder, and that's where it starts. You must believe that God is a rewarder. If you don't see our Father God as a rewarder then your faith will be very weak, and you will find yourself staying in the thirtyfold return bracket.

Joshua 1:8 teaches:

> *This Book of the Law shall not depart from your mouth, but you shall meditate in it day and night, that you may observe to do according to all that is written in it. For then you will make your way prosperous, and then you will have good success."* (NKJV)

If you want to find yourselves prosperous and successful, then meditate on God's Word. Meditation produces activators, and activators stimulate the spiritual realm, initiating the realization of God's promises.

This is what I experienced as I studied the Bible on the subject of tithes and tithing. As I began to grow in understanding, God's Word began to grow inside of me, and I became more fruitful. The understanding of my confession gave me more faith. The

MEDITATION PRODUCES ACTIVATORS, AND ACTIVATORS STIMULATE THE SPIRITUAL REALM, INITIATING THE REALIZATION OF GOD'S PROMISES!

Faith for the Hundredfold Return

Scriptures working in me started activating a process in my life, producing blessing. And my meditation stimulated me to live out biblical principles.

As I was meditating and living out these principles, I noticed that I had collected an entire notebook full of scriptures that were building my faith concerning giving and receiving. I came to call these scriptures "activators."

The definition for the word *activators* is "the ingredients used to stimulate or initiate a process."[1] The Bible is full of activators meant for us to use for every issue of life. It is our job to find and activate them. Once you start confessing the activators with understanding and faith, this will stimulate or initiate a process, and this process will produce the perfect will of God in your life.

This is how Jesus defeated the devil in the wilderness through every temptation. When the devil tempted Him to turn stones into bread, Jesus responded:

> *Man shall not live by bread alone but by every word that proceedeth out of the mouth of God.*
> Matthew 4:4

---
1. Dictionary.com

ONCE YOU START CONFESSING THE ACTIVATORS WITH UNDERSTANDING AND FAITH, THIS WILL STIMULATE OR INITIATE A PROCESS, AND THIS PROCESS WILL PRODUCE THE PERFECT WILL OF GOD IN YOUR LIFE!

Faith for the Hundredfold Return

Jesus was quoting Deuteronomy 8:3:

> *So He humbled you, allowed you to hunger, and fed you with manna which you did not know nor did your fathers know, that He might make you know that man shall not live by bread alone; but man lives by every word that proceeds from the mouth of the LORD.* (NKJV)

Deuteronomy 8 teaches us to be humble and not trust in our own ability, but in the Word of God. This is a fundamental principle of our faith. By meditating on this scripture, I understood how it gave Jesus strength in that moment of weakness. It activated His faith to trust in the Father to sustain Him and not rely on His own ability.

If you want to live a victorious life, you need these activators working in you. Here is a testimony from one of my friends:

After returning home one day, he found that his shed had been broken into, several of his tools were missing, and those particular tools were very important to his current job. He and his wife started praying over the situation. They were led by the Spirit to confess the promise of Malachi

3:11, that because of our tithes, God will rebuke the devourer for our sake.

In this way, they activated God's authority over the situation. The following day a neighbor brought all those tools back and apologized, saying that his younger brother had visited his house and had stolen their belongings.

Malachi 3:11 gave this brother the faith to speak to his present circumstance and declare God's authority over the situation. Because he had activators in his heart, he was able to stimulate his faith, and the result was a return of everything he had lost.

I want to challenge you to begin to collect your own activators. Buy a notebook and write on the front cover ACTIVATORS. Then, use that notebook to document your personal activators, as the Holy Spirit reveals them to you. I promise you will not be disappointed. Now, again we are going deeper to discover the power of *Living in God's Economy.*

Chapter 5

ACTIVATORS

Now that we have looked at our motive, heart, and faith, we are ready to start activating God's favor over our lives. The following scriptures are what I call ACTIVATORS. These are, in fact, the very activators I have personally stood on and that have made all the difference in my life.

Activators, again, are "the ingredients that stimulate or initiate a process."[1] Some of these activators are life principles for you to start applying today, while some are the Father's promises for you to start confessing over yourself for the days ahead. Like a doctor giving you the remedy for a disease, this is your cure to start living in God's economy.

---

1. Dictionary.com

Each one of the following activators came from my study of God's Word as I prepared for my Sunday morning tithe messages. The messages came from more than five years of receiving the offering on Sunday mornings. As I mentioned in the beginning of the book, I reluctantly took up the task the pastor requested of me, God helped me, and these are the messages the Father weighed on my heart for the Sunday morning tithe messages. They have transformed my life, and today I walk in the favor of God. Try them out for yourself!

My Personal Activators

(If they speak to you, use them.)

— Faithful Stewardship —

Luke 16:10-12

Whoever can be trusted with very little can also be trusted with much, and whoever is dishonest with very little will also be dishonest with much. So if you have not been trustworthy in handling worldly wealth, who will trust you with true riches? And if you have not been trustworthy with someone else's property, who will give you property of your own?

No one can serve two masters. Either you will hate the one and love the other, or you will be devoted to the one and despise the other. You cannot serve both God and money. (NIV)

Luke 16 is telling us to be a good steward of our earthly wealth. One aspect of having wealth is a test of stewardship. How you handle money defines your stewardship, faithful or otherwise.

ACTIVATORS

The Pharisees scoffed at Jesus when He told the Parable of the Shrewd Manager (see Luke 16) because they loved their money. Tithing crucifies our flesh and teaches us to be loyal stewards.

Verse 11 is very sobering. How I handle worldly wealth limits the true riches being given to me. I want God to trust me with His riches, so I need to learn how to be a good steward of worldly wealth Tithing frees me from the danger of worldly wealth becoming my master and places God as my Provider.

I see worldly wealth as something God has entrusted me with to be a blessing. I steward my wealth into three categories: Family, Kingdom Building, and Showing God's Love to Others. How about you?

TITHING FREES ME FROM THE DANGER OF WORLDLY WEALTH BECOMING MY MASTER AND PLACES GOD AS MY PROVIDER!

— The Fear of God —

Deuteronomy 14:22-23
Thou shalt truly tithe all the increase of thy seed, that the field bringeth forth year by year. And thou shalt eat before the LORD thy God, in the place which he shall choose to place his name there, the tithe of thy corn, of thy wine, and of thine oil, and the firstlings of thy herds and of thy flocks; that thou mayest learn to fear the LORD thy God always.

Tithing teaches us to fear God. This is the number one guiding principle in my life. This is not a bad fear, but a Daddy kind of fear, a healthy respect. When you were growing up, you feared Dad's punishment if you broke his rules, and that is not a bad fear to have. It kept you from making many mistakes.

It's the same with our heavenly Father. Having the fear of God in our life keeps us form making serious mistakes. It is foolish to be arrogant against an all-powerful loving God. Here are a few scriptures of the blessing that follows one who learns to fear God:

Psalm 128:1-6

How joyful are those who fear the LORD—
all who follow his ways!
You will enjoy the fruit of your labor.
How joyful and prosperous you will be!
Your wife will be like a fruitful grapevine,
flourishing within your home.
Your children will be like vigorous young olive trees
as they sit around your table.
That is the LORD's blessing
for those who fear him.
May the LORD continually bless you from Zion.
May you see Jerusalem prosper as long as you live.
May you live to enjoy your grandchildren.
May Israel have peace!. (NLT)

ACTIVATORS

Psalm 34:7-9

The angel of the Lord encampeth round about them that fear him and delivereth them. O taste and see that the Lord is good: blessed is the man that trusteth in him. O fear the Lord, ye his saints: for there is no want to them that fear him.

Proverbs 9:10-11

The fear of the Lord is the beginning of wisdom: and the knowledge of the holy is understanding. For by me thy days shall be multiplied, and the years of thy life shall be increased.

Proverbs 22:4

By humility and the fear of the Lord are riches, and honour, and life.

Tithing teaches us to put God first, to reverence and honor Him, respecting and recognizing Him as the higher authority in our life. This is a very healthy attitude to have.

TITHING TEACHES US TO PUT GOD FIRST, TO REVERENCE AND HONOR HIM, RESPECTING AND RECOGNIZING HIM AS THE HIGHER AUTHORITY IN OUR LIFE!

— Wait on God's Perfect Timing —

Deuteronomy 9:9-11

When I [Moses} was gone up into the mount to receive the tables of stone, even the tables of the covenant which the LORD made with you, then I abode in the mount forty days and forty nights, I neither did eat bread nor drink water. And the LORD delivered unto me two tables of stone written with the finger of God; and on them was written according to all the words, which the LORD spake with you in the mount out of the midst of the fire in the day of the assembly. And it came to pass at the end of forty days and forty nights, that the LORD gave me the two tables of stone, even the tables of the covenant.

When you go to God about any situation, don't be discouraged if you don't see the results right away. God is working in your life, but He does it in His perfect timing. Are you willing, like Moses, to wait for God's plan for your life?

Moses was so desperate for God's will that for forty days he trusted Him for the needs of his physical body. Ask yourself, "Is God's plan worth the wait?"

MOSES WAS SO DESPERATE FOR GOD'S WILL THAT FOR FORTY DAYS HE TRUSTED HIM FOR THE NEEDS OF HIS PHYSICAL BODY!

— Remember, It Is God —

Deuteronomy 8:18
> *But thou shalt remember the L*ORD *thy God: for it is he that giveth thee power to get wealth, that he may establish his covenant which he swore unto thy fathers, as it is this day.*

Remind yourself that it is God who is prospering you. Tithing is giving back to God what He has already given to us. This reminds me where my resources come from and what my responsibilities with them arew.

— Five Loaves and Two Fish —

John 6:9-13

There is a lad here, which hath five barley loaves, and two small fishes: but what are they among so many?

And Jesus said, Make the men sit down.

Now there was much grass in the place. So, the men sat down, in number about five thousand. And Jesus took the loaves; and when he had given thanks, he distributed to the disciples, and the disciples to them that were set down; and likewise of the fishes as much as they would.

When they were filled, he said unto his disciples, Gather up the fragments that remain, that nothing be lost. Therefore, they gathered them together, and filled twelve baskets with the fragments of the five barley loaves, which remained over and above unto them that had eaten.

LIVING IN GOD'S ECONOMY

I can imagine this young boy, walking around with a big smile on his face, knowing that it was his giving that resulted in Jesus feeding the five thousand. It was because of his giving that thousands were able to hear the Gospel. God is doing that same thing with your tithes. He is taking your giving and using it to feed the multitude.

Of course, Jesus didn't need that little boy's five loaves and two fish. He could have done it some other way. But He permitted the boy to be a partaker in His glory. This thought blows me away. God is giving us an opportunity to be partakers in His glory by willingly giving of our mortal wealth.

Like the disciples said to Jesus, *"What are they* {the five barley loaves, and two small fish] *among so many?"* (verse 9). In the same way, what can we do today about such an overwhelming lost community? But God uses our willingness to release His glory, and we get to become partakers in the salvation of the lost. What a great honor!

Tithing is an opportunity to be a part of feeding the five thousand so that they can hear the Gospel.

THIS THOUGHT BLOWS ME AWAY. GOD IS GIVING US AN OPPORTUNITY TO BE PARTAKERS IN HIS GLORY BY WILLINGLY GIVING OF OUR MORTAL WEALTH!

GOD USES OUR WILLINGNESS TO RELEASE HIS GLORY, AND WE GET TO BECOME PARTAKERS IN THE SALVATION OF THE LOST. WHAT A GREAT HONOR!

— Where Is Your Treasure? —

Luke 12:16-21

And he spake a parable unto them, saying, The ground of a certain rich man brought forth plentifully. And he thought within himself, saying, What shall I do, because I have no room where to bestow my fruits? And he said, This will I do: I will pull down my barns, and build greater; and there will I bestow all my fruits and my goods. And I will say to my soul, Soul, thou hast much goods laid up for many years; take thine ease, eat, drink, and be merry.

But God said unto him, Thou fool, this night thy soul shall be required of thee: then whose shall those things be, which thou hast provided? So is he that layeth up treasure for himself and is not rich toward God.

LIVING IN GOD'S ECONOMY

We can get so caught up in this life, working to obtain wealth, that we don't do anything for God. Jesus called that kind of life *"foolish."* What will it profit a man to gain the whole world? You can't take it with you.

I would rather be rich in eternity and poor on earth than poor in eternity and rich on earth.

I WOULD RATHER BE RICH IN ETERNITY AND POOR ON EARTH THAN POOR IN ETERNITY AND RICH ON EARTH!

— Where Are You Investing? —

Matthew 6:19-21

Lay not up for yourselves treasures upon earth, where moth and rust doth corrupt, and where thieves break through and steal. But lay up for yourselves treasures in heaven, where neither moth nor rust doth corrupt, and where thieves do not break through nor steal: for where your treasure is, there will your heart be also.

Tithing is storing up treasure in Heaven.

— Don't Compare Yourself To the Wicked —

Malachi 3:13-15
"You have spoken arrogantly against me," says the LORD. "Yet you ask, 'What have we said against you?' "You have said, 'It is futile to serve God. What do we gain by carrying out his requirements and going about like mourners before the LORD Almighty? But now we call the arrogant blessed. Certainly evildoers prosper, and even when they put God to the test, they get away with it.'" (NIV)

We need to be careful not to envy the success of the wicked and say in our heart, "The ungodly are blessed. What benefit is it to obey God?" This is a lie from the devil, and you should reject it and not allow it to take hold of your heart.

"What benefit is it to obey God?" This is a lie from the devil, and you should reject it and not allow it to take hold of your heart!

ACTIVATORS

The entirety of Psalm 37 deals with this thought:

*Never envy the wicked! Soon they fade away like grass and disappear. Trust in the L*ORD *instead. Be kind and good to others; then you will live safely here in the land and prosper, feeding in safety.*
*Be delighted with the L*ORD*. Then he will give you all your heart's desires. Commit everything you do to the L*ORD*. Trust him to help you do it, and he will. Your innocence will be clear to everyone. He will vindicate you with the blazing light of justice shining down as from the noonday sun.*
*Rest in the L*ORD*; wait patiently for him to act. Do not be envious of evil men who prosper.*
*Stop your anger! Turn off your wrath. Do not fret and worry—it only leads to harm. For the wicked shall be destroyed, but those who trust the L*ORD *shall be given every blessing. Only a little while and the wicked shall disappear. You will look for them in vain. But all who humble themselves before the L*ORD *shall be given every blessing and shall have wonderful peace.*

LIVING IN GOD'S ECONOMY

*The L*ORD *is laughing at those who plot against the godly, for he knows their judgment day is coming. Evil men take aim to slay the poor; they are ready to butcher those who do right. But their swords will be plunged into their own hearts, and all their weapons will be broken.*

*It is better to have little and be godly than to own an evil man's wealth; for the strength of evil men shall be broken, but the L*ORD *takes care of those he has forgiven.*

*Day by day the L*ORD *observes the good deeds done by godly men, and gives them eternal rewards. He cares for them when times are hard; even in famine, they will have enough. But evil men shall perish. These enemies of God will wither like grass and disappear like smoke. Evil men borrow and "cannot pay it back"! But the good man returns what he owes with some extra besides. Those blessed by the L*ORD *shall inherit the earth, but those cursed by him shall die.*

*The steps of good men are directed by the L*ORD. *He delights in each step they take. If they fall, it isn't fatal, for the L*ORD *holds them with his hand.*

*I have been young and now I am old. And in all my years I have never seen the L*ORD *forsake a*

ACTIVATORS

man who loves him; nor have I seen the children of the godly go hungry. Instead, the godly are able to be generous with their gifts and loans to others, and their children are a blessing.

So if you want an eternal home, leave your evil, low-down ways and live good lives. For the LORD loves justice and fairness; he will never abandon his people. They will be kept safe forever; but all who love wickedness shall perish.

The godly shall be firmly planted in the land and live there forever. The godly man is a good counselor because he is just and fair and knows right from wrong.

Evil men spy on the godly, waiting for an excuse to accuse them and then demanding their death. But the LORD will not let these evil men succeed, nor let the godly be condemned when they are brought before the judge.

Don't be impatient for the LORD to act! Keep traveling steadily along his pathway and in due season he will honor you with every blessing, and you will see the wicked destroyed. I myself have seen it happen: a proud and evil man, towering like a cedar of Lebanon, but when I looked again, he was gone! I searched but could not find

> *him! But the good man—what a different story! For the good man—the blameless, the upright, the man of peace—he has a wonderful future ahead of him. For him there is a happy ending. But evil men shall be destroyed, and their posterity shall be cut off.*
>
> *The LORD saves the godly! He is their salvation and their refuge when trouble comes. Because they trust in him, he helps them and delivers them from the plots of evil men.* (TLB)

Amen! What more needs to be said?

— God's Blessings Strengthens My Heart —

Psalm 27:13-14
I had fainted unless I had believed to see the goodness of the LORD in the land of the living. Wait on the LORD: be of good courage, and he shall strengthen thine heart: wait, I say, on the LORD.

King David makes a great point here. We need to see God's goodness in our present life. It is a fact that we are human and need encouragement. Encouragement strengthens our heart. That is why hearing testimonies of God blessing other people brings us victory. It gives us the strength to fight on.

Why not have a notebook to keep a record of your own testimonies, to remind yourself of God's goodness in your life?

Why not have a notebook to keep a record of your own testimonies, to remind yourself of God's goodness in your life?

— Honey in the Rock —

Psalm 81:16
He should have fed them also with the finest of the wheat: and with honey out of the rock should I have satisfied thee.

God desires to give us the finest, the very desires of our heart. He is a good Father who delights in giving to His children. We hinder Him through our disobedience.

I feel the same about my children; I would rather bless them than punish them. How could God do any less?

God desires to give us the finest, the very desires of our heart. He is a good Father who delights in giving to His children. We hinder Him through our disobedience!

— Father's Life Advice —

Proverbs 4:10-13

Hear O my son and receive my sayings; and the years of thy life shall be many. I have taught thee in the way of wisdom; I have led thee in right paths. When thou goest, thy steps shall not be straitened; and when thou runnest, thou shalt not stumble. Take fast hold of instruction; let her not go: keep her; for she is thy life.

God is a good Father who is teaching me the ways of wisdom. There's a very good reason He is asking us to be tithers. He is teaching us a wisdom that makes our paths straight. Hold fast to His instructions, for they are good. They hold the keys to life.

— Don't Rob God —

Malachi 3:8

Will a man rob God? Yet ye have robbed me. But ye say, Wherein have we robbed thee? In tithes and offerings.

A businessman wanted to give his three employees an end-of-the-year bonus. He called them in and said, "I am giving you each $100 to get me a pizza. After getting me a pizza, you may keep the remaining money."

The first employee said to himself, "I deserve this whole $100 for myself." So, he kept all the money and didn't buy his boss any pizza. The second employee decided, "I will buy a cheap microwavable pizza so I can keep more money for myself." The third employee purchased the best pizza Papa Johns had to offer and added in some bread sticks.

ACTIVATORS

The following day the businessman called the employees in and revealed his plan. He wanted to give each of them an end-of-the-year bonus. This bonus would be a percentage of their annual salary, and what would determine the percentage was how much they had spent on the pizza.

This is an example of how we treat God —good or bad — with our tithes. Our prosperity is a result of the blessings of God over our lives, and He requires only 10% of what He has blessed us with. Our 10% is for God's pizza, not for us to keep for ourselves.

Our prosperity is a result of the blessings of God over our lives, and He requires only 10% of what He has blessed us with!

— What Are You Confessing? —

Numbers 14:26-28

And the LORD spake unto Moses and unto Aaron, saying, How long shall I bear with this evil congregation, which murmur against me? I have heard the murmurings of the children of Israel, which they murmur against me. Say unto them, As truly as I live, saith the LORD, as ye have spoken in mine ears, so will I do to you.

Complaining about present issues and not trusting God for the future will rob you of the blessing He wants to pour out in your life. Check yourself before you wreck yourself. Your confession might become your reality.

Repent of your negative outlook and begin to trust that God is working all things for your good.

— Giving To Missionaries —

Philippians 4:14-19

Not withstanding ye have well done, that ye did communicate with my affliction. Now ye Philippians know also, that in the beginning of the gospel, when I departed from Macedonia, no church communicated with me as concerning giving and receiving, but ye only. For even in Thessalonica ye sent once and again unto my necessity. Not because I desire a gift: but I desire fruit that may abound to your account. But I have all, and abound: I am full, having received of Epaphroditus the things which were sent from you, an odour of a sweet smell, a sacrifice acceptable, wellpleasing to God. But my God shall supply all your need according to his riches in glory by Christ Jesus.

ACTIVATORS

The Philippian church was sending financial support to Paul, and Paul said that, because of their giving, they had communicated with his affliction. In other words, they had become partakers together with Paul's labor. According to verse 17, this act of love was increasing their heavenly account. Even though you might not be a pastor or a missionary, you are a partner with the labor of those you support financially, and their accomplishments are added to your eternal rewards.

Paul described our giving as *"an odour of a sweet smell, a sacrifice acceptable, wellpleasing to God."* John wrote:

3 John 1:5-8
Dear friend, you are doing a good work for God in taking care of the traveling teachers and missionaries who are passing through. They have told the church here of your friendship and your loving deeds. I am glad when you send them on their way with a generous gift. For they are traveling for the Lord and take neither food, clothing, shelter, nor money from those who are not Christians, even though they have preached to them. So we ourselves should take care of them in order that we may become partners with them in the Lord's work. (TLB)

— The Blessing of the Tithe —

Malachi 3:10-12
> *Bring ye all the tithes into the storehouse, that there may be meat in mine house, and prove me now herewith, saith the L*ORD *of hosts, if I will not open you the windows of heaven, and pour you out a blessing, that there shall not be room enough to receive it. And I will rebuke the devourer for your sakes, and he shall not destroy the fruits of your ground; neither shall your vine cast her fruit before the time in the field, saith the L*ORD *of hosts. And all nations shall call you blessed: for ye shall be a delightsome land, saith the L*ORD *of hosts.*

God is saying, "Let Me prove to you how much I want to bless you." One thing I have learned about God is that He loves blessing His children. If we know how to give good gifts to our children, how

ACTIVATORS

much more does our heavenly Father (see Matthew 7:11 and Luke 11:13). It is only disobedience that stops His blessings.

God intends for us to have the finest life can offer, and there is no limit to His ability to prosper you. We are the ones who limit Him. Once we get our motive, heart, and obedience right, God's favor will shine on us.

There are three blessings that come with obedience to the tithe. First, an open window of blessing pouring into your life, so much that there is not enough room to receive it. Second, a financial protection over the fruit of your labor. Third, your home will become *"a delightsome land."* How awesome is that?

GOD INTENDS FOR US TO HAVE THE FINEST LIFE CAN OFFER, AND THERE IS NO LIMIT TO HIS ABILITY TO PROSPER YOU. WE ARE THE ONES WHO LIMIT HIM!

— God Is a Rewarder —

Hebrews 11:6
But without faith it is impossible to please Him, for he who comes to God must believe that He is, and that He is a rewarder of those who diligently seek Him. (NKJV)

It starts here. You must believe that God is a rewarder. If you don't see our Father God as a rewarder, then your faith will be very weak, and you will be stuck with a thirtyfold return. Believe for the greater increase.

— Honor God with Your Possessions —

Proverbs 3:9-10
Honor the LORD with your possessions,
And with the firstfruits of all your increase;
So your barns will be filled with plenty,
And your vats will overflow with new wine.
(NKJV)

Have you ever thought of your tithes as a means of showing honor to our Father? You are recognizing His authority. Abraham paid tithes to Melchizedek, recognizing him as high priest of the Most High. He was recognizing Melchizedek's authority and position. Doing this will open the window of Heaven and pour out blessings upon your finances. God guarantees it.

— God Is Directing My Path —

Proverbs 3:5-6

Trust in the LORD with all thine heart; and lean not unto thine own understanding. In all thy ways acknowledge him, and he shall direct thy paths.

Tithing is putting your trust in God as your Provider and not leaning on your own understanding. When you put your trust in Him to provide, He leads your paths to true prosperity.

— The Blessing of Sufficiency! —

2 Corinthians 9:6-8

But this I say: He who sows sparingly will also reap sparingly, and he who sows bountifully will also reap bountifully. So let each one give as he purposes in his heart, not grudgingly or of necessity; for God loves a cheerful giver. And God is able to make all grace abound toward you, that you, always having all sufficiency in all things, may have an abundance for every good work.
(NKJV)

Your giving is rewarded with the blessing of sufficiency. That signifies a perfect condition of life in which no aid or support is any longer needed. You will be content with all things.

Have you ever been around someone who seemed to always have blessings being given to them? If so, it's because these people are givers.

ACTIVATORS

They are always giving, and if you sell them something for $100, they give you $200 for it. Generous givers reap abundantly because they have learned never to sow sparingly. How about you?

Your giving is rewarded with the blessing of sufficiency. That signifies a perfect condition of life in which no aid or support is any longer needed!

GENEROUS GIVERS
REAP ABUNDANTLY
BECAUSE THEY HAVE
LEARNED NEVER TO
SOW SPARINGLY!

— Spiritual Farmers —

2 Corinthians 9:10-14

For God is the one who provides seed for the farmer and then bread to eat. In the same way, he will provide and increase your resources and then produce a great harvest of generosity in you. Yes, you will be enriched in every way so that you can always be generous. And when we take your gifts to those who need them, they will thank God. So two good things will result from this ministry of giving—the needs of the believers in Jerusalem will be met, and they will joyfully express their thanks to God.

As a result of your ministry, they will give glory to God. For your generosity to them and to all believers will prove that you are obedient to the Good News of Christ. And they will pray for you with deep affection because of the overflowing grace God has given to you. (NLT)

ACTIVATORS

Givers to God's Kingdom are spiritual farmers. When you become a spiritual farmer, God gives you seed to sow. The more you sow, the more seed God will give you. As a farmer reaps a harvest to eat, you will reap spiritual fruit for eternity.

When you become a spiritual farmer, God gives you seed to sow. The more you sow, the more seed God will give you!

— My God —

Philippians 4:19
But my God shall supply all your need according to his riches in glory by Christ Jesus.

When we are living in God's economy, the issues of this world no longer affect us. Why? Because all of my needs are supplied by **MY GOD**. What more needs to be said?

— God's Law —

Luke 6:38

Give, and it shall be given unto you; good measure, pressed down, and shaken together, and running over, shall men give into your bosom. For with the same measure that ye mete withal it shall be measured to you again.

If you give, it always comes back to you. This is one of God's unchanging laws that He has established in the earth.

If you give, it always comes back to you. This is one of God's unchanging laws that He has established in the earth!

— The Widow's Offering —

Mark 12:41-44

Jesus sat down near the collection box in the Temple and watched as the crowds dropped in their money. Many rich people put in large amounts. Then a poor widow came and dropped in two small coins. Jesus called his disciples to him and said, "I tell you the truth, this poor widow has given more than all the others who are making contributions. For they gave a tiny part of their surplus, but she, poor as she is, has given everything she had to live on." (NLT)

The fact that this woman's offering caught Jesus' attention speaks volumes of the value He places on giving. God is judging the intent of our heart in giving not the amount we give. It takes more faith to give when you have little, but when you are faithful with the little, God can bless you with more.

IT TAKES MORE FAITH TO GIVE WHEN YOU HAVE LITTLE, BUT WHEN YOU ARE FAITHFUL WITH THE LITTLE, GOD CAN BLESS YOU WITH MORE!

— Content with Whatever —

Philippians 4:11-13
> *Not that I was ever in need, for I have learned how to be content with whatever I have. I know how to live on almost nothing or with everything. I have learned the secret of living in every situation, whether it is with a full stomach or empty, with plenty or little. For I can do everything through Christ, who gives me strength.* (NLT)

It is God who gives us strength. Find happiness in what you have, and don't be like the children of Israel who complained.

— Seek First the Kingdom and God's Righteousness —

Matthew 6:31-34
So don't worry at all about having enough food and clothing. Why be like the heathen? For they take pride in all these things and are deeply concerned about them. But your heavenly Father already knows perfectly well that you need them, and he will give them to you if you give him first place in your life and live as he wants you to. So don't be anxious about tomorrow. God will take care of your tomorrow too. Live one day at a time. (TLB)

God knows you have need of things. Put your focus on the Kingdom, and these things will be added unto you. If you are faithful to God today, He will take care of your tomorrows.

IF YOU ARE FAITHFUL TO GOD TODAY, HE WILL TAKE CARE OF YOUR TOMORROWS!

— God Has a Plan for You —

Jeremiah 29:11
For I know the plans I have for you, says the LORD. They are plans for good and not for evil, to give you a future and a hope.

God has a future for you. Trusting Him with your tithes and offerings is trusting His plan.

GOD HAS A FUTURE FOR YOU. TRUSTING HIM WITH YOUR TITHES AND OFFERINGS IS TRUSTING HIS PLAN!

— Don't Observe the Wind —

Ecclesiastes 11:4-6

He that observeth the wind shall not sow; and he that regardeth the clouds shall not reap. As thou knowest not what is the way of the spirit, nor how the bones do grow in the womb of her that is with child: even so thou knowest not the works of God who maketh all. In the morning sow thy seed, and in the evening withhold not thine hand: for thou knowest not whether shall prosper, either this or that, or whether they both shall be alike good

If you wait for perfect conditions, you will never sow. We can't know what God is doing with the seed we are planting. Trust Him!

WE CAN'T KNOW WHAT GOD IS DOING WITH THE SEED WE ARE PLANTING. TRUST HIM!

— You Are Not Forsaken —

Psalm 37:25
I have been young, and now am old; yet have I not seen the righteous forsaken, nor his seed begging bread.

God never forsakes His children, and we, therefore, are never left begging. Never forget: you are a child of God and an heir of His Kingdom.

GOD NEVER FORSAKES HIS CHILDREN, AND WE, THEREFORE, ARE NEVER LEFT BEGGING!

— Follow the Blesser —

Luke 5:1-11

One day as he [Jesus] was preaching on the shore of Lake Gennesaret, great crowds pressed in on him to listen to the Word of God. He noticed two empty boats standing at the water's edge while the fishermen washed their nets. Stepping into one of the boats, Jesus asked Simon, its owner, to push out a little into the water, so that he could sit in the boat and speak to the crowds from there.

When he had finished speaking, he said to Simon, "Now go out where it is deeper and let down your nets and you will catch a lot of fish!"

"Sir," Simon replied, "we worked hard all last night and didn't catch a thing. But if you say so, we'll try again."

And this time their nets were so full that they began to tear! A shout for help brought their partners in the other boat, and soon both boats were filled with fish and on the verge of sinking. When Simon Peter realized what had happened, he fell to his knees before Jesus and said, "Oh, sir, please leave us—I'm too much of a sinner for you to have around." For he was awestruck by the size of their catch, as were the others with him, and his partners too—James and John, the sons of Zebedee.

Jesus replied, "Don't be afraid! From now on you'll be fishing for the souls of men!"

And as soon as they landed, they left everything and went with him. (TLB)

What I like about this story is that after Jesus had prospered Simon beyond anything he could possibly contain, Simon left all that prosperity and followed Jesus. I want to be like Simon and follow the Blesser and not the blessing.

I WANT TO BE LIKE SIMON AND FOLLOW THE BLESSER AND NOT THE BLESSING!

Chapter 6

CONCLUSION

I have made this book as short and straightforward as I possibly could so that it would be an easy read and very applicable. My goal is that you use it as a resource to continue to build your faith. Start meditating on these activators and start confessing them over your life. This is taking up the shield of faith, so that you can quench all the fiery darts of the evil one (see Ephesians 6:16). Let the Word of God renew your mind so that you can walk in the fullness of God's plan for your life.

I encourage you to be honest with yourself and define your motives. Search where your heart is and begin to start building your faith. When you make these changes, you will be lining yourself up with God's favor.

LIVING IN GOD'S ECONOMY

A bodybuilder goes to the gym day after day. He does not become a massive weight lifter after a single workout. His growth is from dedicated effort year after year. The same is true with building your faith. Don't expect to have faith to move mountains if you have never moved a little hill. Exercise your faith just as a bodybuilder does. That is what's so great about tithing; it is an exercise of your faith.

Now that you have read the entire book, I encourage you to go back and take each chapter as a stage. Once you get Chapter 1 rooted and established in your life, then you will be prepared for your next stage. Move on to Chapter 2, like a bodybuilder adding another weight to the bar. You are learning to lean not on your own understanding but acknowledging God's. You are now living a God-directed life.

Even though I have written this book, I am still growing in this area. I continue to exercise my faith and am constantly learning to apply God's Word over my life. The more I grow in this area, the more victorious I am becoming.

While writing this, I experienced a great attack of the enemy against my faith. I won't go into

CONCLUSION

the details, but fear overcame me so that I began to even lose sleep. Whenever we begin to grow, the enemy comes against us in a greater way. He doesn't want you to realize the authority you can walk in, and he will do his best to discourage you.

Remember, we wrestle against principalities, against powers, against rulers of the darkness of this world, and against spiritual wickedness in high places (see Ephesians 6:12). The Word of God is our sword. Use it wisely to fight against these dark forces. As we confess God's Word, we are destroying the efforts of the evil one against us.

I broke through this attack by seeking prayer from someone I knew would take my request serious. Then I started confessing God's Word over myself and my life. The devil loves to put lies in your mind. You have to say, "No, that's not true, because God's Word says … ."

I have found that sometimes you need to have another believer join in the fight with you. One will cast out a thousand, but two will cast out ten thousand (see Deuteronomy 32:30). Sometimes it seems that you are outnumbered by the enemy. Because of this, it's important to build relationships with other believers who are willing to do battle with you and for you.

The most import thing that helped me overcome the enemy was my confession. Because I had hidden God's Word in my heart, the Holy Spirit was able to bring it to my remembrance, allowing me to stand in that difficult time. Not only are we learning to walk in God's favor, but also in His authority. I implore you to take up this mantle and apply God's Word over your life. Soon you will see God's goodness running after you. Why? Because He is faithful, and He is good. Experience knowing God as the Rewarder.

As you are finishing this book, I would like to pray this prayer over you:

> *I thank You, Father, that as this believer takes up this mantle and starts applying Your Word over their life, they will see Your goodness. I thank You that Your goodness is running after them because of who You are, not because of what we do. You are a faithful God, and You are good. I thank You, therefore, that they will experience You as a Rewarder in ways they have not before.*
> *Amen!*

About the Author

Jeremy Voisin was born and raised in a Christian home in South Louisiana. While he was young, his parents attended various churches and then started a small church. At the time, Jeremy was in his early youth, and the influence of the world caused him to be very rebellious throughout his teen years. He is now very ashamed of the person he became in those years. You might say that he lived out the story of the prodigal son, doing things he now regrets.

It was at the age of twenty-five that Jeremy finally realized how much of a mess he had made of his life and how much he needed God, fully surrendered to God and to God's plan for his life. At the age of twenty-eight he started a local outreach ministry, hosting youth rallies. By the age of thirty-six, he began teaching in his father's church, which, by that time, had grown to be one of the largest churches in the area. Today Vision Christian Center in Bourg, Louisiana, still stands as the largest Foursquare church in the district.

It was the invitation to Jeremy to begin giving a five-minute message on tithing during the Sunday morning services at Vision Christian Center that God used to begin a work in him that would eventually result in this, his first book. Jeremy is now a licensed and ordained minister through the International Church of the Foursquare Gospel. Over the years, he has been through many trials that challenged him to his core, but every challenge has helped him to mature in the wisdom of God and to grow to where he is today.

Jeremy has been happily married for sixteen years to his beautiful wife, and together they have the honor to raise and guide their five children. While he is currently doing ministry, his heart is to continue to grow in his relationship with the Father and be willing to be used in whatever capacity he is needed in God's Kingdom.

Author Contact Page

You may contact Jeremy Voisin directly at:

jvoisin79@gmail.com

www.ingramcontent.com/pod-product-compliance
Lightning Source LLC
Chambersburg PA
CBHW032136040426
42449CB00005B/275